STARS, CLUSTERS AND GALAXIES

THE YOUNG STARGAZER'S GUIDE TO THE GALAXY

BY JOHN GUSTAFSON

JULIAN MESSNER

Library of Congress Cataloging-in-Publication Data

Gustafson, John R.
    Stars, clusters and galaxies / by John R. Gustafson.
        p.   cm — (The young stargazer's guide to the galaxy)
    Includes index
    Summary: Describes stars, star clusters, galaxies, and other
objects in the universe and how to find them with the naked
eye, binoculars, or a telescope.
    1. Astronomy—Observers' manuals—Juvenile literature.
2. Milky Way—Observers' manuals—Juvenile literature.
3. Stars—Observers' manuals—Juvenile literature. [1. Stars. 2.
Astronomy—Observers' manuals. 3. Constellations.]   I. Title.
II. Series.
QB64.G87   1992   92-11228
523.8'022'3—dc20   CIP
                                                    AC

ISBN 0-671-72536-X (LSB)
ISBN 0-671-72537-8 (pbk.)

Copyright © 1992 by RGA Publishing Group, Inc.

Published by Julian Messner, a division of Simon & Schuster,
Simon and Schuster Building, Rockefeller Center,
1230 Avenue of the Americas, New York, NY 10020.

Produced by: RGA Publishing Group, Inc.
Project Editors: Lisa Melton and Barbara Russiello
Design: Heidi Frieder and Virginia Pope
Cover design: Virginia Pope
Illustrations: Mark Brest van Kempen
Photo credits on page 62

Manufactured in the United States of America
10   9   8   7   6   5   4   3   2

**To my father, one of the real stars
of the universe.**

**Special thanks to John Hodge
for proposing the book
and sticking with it.**

CONTENTS

This beautiful reflection nebula, NGC 1977, is the northernmost star in the sword of Orion.

THE UNIVERSE AT OUR DOORSTEP

Nearly every point of light you see when you look up at the night sky is created by another star similar to the Sun. Most of the stars we see are much more powerful than the Sun, but they are so far away that they appear only as small dots of light.

The night sky is also the doorway to a much greater variety of celestial objects. A few of the points of light we see are not stars. With a pair of binoculars or a small telescope, you can view not only the stars, but also many other objects not visible to the naked eye. Such objects include star clusters, in which thousands of stars travel together; hot clouds of gas that shine with a ghostly glow; black clouds of dust so thick that they block the light of thousands of stars behind them; and the scattered remains of stars that died in violent explosions.

All of these sights can be seen in the night sky. With a little effort, you can learn how to find the points of light that have especially interesting stories to tell and how to understand what you are seeing. Let's first consider what types of objects exist near us in space.

WHAT IS A STAR?

The Sun is a good example of a typical **star.** Our Sun is a ball of gas that's about a million miles across and weighs a billion billion billion tons (that's 1,000,000,000,000,000,000,000,000,000 tons!). It also emits light because it is so hot. The Sun is about 10,000 degrees Fahrenheit on the surface and millions of degrees at the center. The hottest stars known are about 100,000 degrees at

the surface and shine with a white-hot fury. The diameters of these stars are about 20 times larger than the Sun's. The coolest stars are about 4,000 degrees at the surface and give off a dim, red glow, like an ember from a fire. Most of the stars that exist are of this cool variety. They are about one-fourth the size of the Sun's diameter, and they live longer than other stars do. None of them, however, can be seen without a telescope. Stars that can be seen with the naked eye are the unusual ones that are bright enough to be seen at great distances.

The power that keeps a star hot and shining is generated at its center. There, gas is squeezed together so tightly and becomes so hot that **nuclear fusion** occurs. In fusion, several small particles are combined, or "fused," into one big particle. In each fusion reaction, only a little bit of material is converted into energy. But in a star like our Sun, millions of these reactions are going on at once. In fact, each second many *tons* of material are converted into energy. That's more energy than human beings have used in a million years.

A star actually begins to shine before it turns on its nuclear furnace. A star forms when a cloud of gas in space begins to collapse because of its own gravity. As the collapsing ball gets smaller and smaller, the gas heats up. The gas ball releases this heat energy as shining light. When the star gets so

Orion is best seen during four months of the year, from December to March.

hot inside that nuclear fusion begins, it no longer needs to shrink to generate more heat. That's when it begins a long, stable life as a true star.

The biggest stars burn up their nuclear fuel at an incredible rate. They are like high-powered race cars that get only a few miles to a gallon. They last only 10 million years or so before they exhaust their fuel and begin to die. Cooler stars, like the Sun, are more like efficient economy cars. The Sun will last 10 billion years, even though it started its life with 15 times less fuel than a big, hot star. Cooler stars, smaller and dimmer than the Sun, are the most economical. Long after the Sun and other stars have used up their fuel and burned out, these red embers will still be glowing.

WHAT IS A BINARY STAR?

As astronomers have studied stars through their telescopes, they have learned that most stars are not alone. In fact, most stars have a companion — another star that is nearby, forming a pair with the first. Such a star pair is called a **binary star** (or **double star**). Star systems with more than two members are called **multiple stars**.

Sometimes what appears in a telescope as a binary star is actually an optical illusion. The two stars appear to us to be almost touching, but they are actually far apart from one another. They just happen to lie in the same direction. Such star

The Big Dipper is easy to find. It is part of the constellation Ursa Major. The binary stars, Mizar and Alcor, are in the middle of the Big Dipper's handle.

"pairs" that only appear to be close together but are not are called optical double stars.

When two stars *are* actually close to each other, they form a true binary star. The two stars (or more, in the case of multiple stars) are locked into orbit around each other by gravity, just as the Earth orbits the Sun under the control of gravity.

How do two stars become attached like this? Astronomers once thought that binary stars are formed when two individual stars wander so close to each other that their gravitational attraction links them together. Space is so vast, however, that it is very unlikely that two stars would ever get close

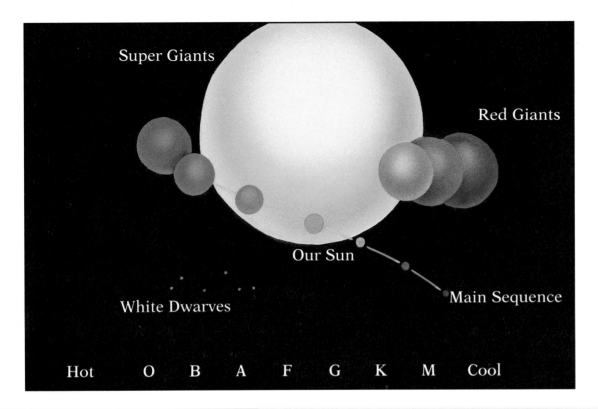

Super Giants

Red Giants

Our Sun

White Dwarves

Main Sequence

Hot　O　B　A　F　G　K　M　Cool

Hot stars are classed O, B, and A. Medium-temperature stars are classed F and G. Cool stars are classed K, M, R, N, and S.

Oily, Baked Aardvark Feet Give Kids Mean, Rotten, Nasty Stomachaches.

TRY THIS ...

USING A MNEMONIC

Astronomers use different letters to designate the different types of stars. The Sun, for example, is called a "G" star.

Originally, astronomers ranked stars according to how bright certain colors were in their light. The list went A, B, C, and so forth. Later, astronomers realized they could determine the temperature of a star by interpreting the colors in the star's light. Rather than relabeling the stars they had studied, astronomers rearranged the list of letters from the hottest stars to the coolest. The order is as follows: O, B, A, F, G, K, M, R, N, S.

To recall the order, astronomers use a memory device called a mnemonic (nih-MON-ik).

They devised a sentence consisting of words whose first letters match the letters of star classes. The sentence handed down by tradition is **Oh Be A Fine Girl, Kiss Me Right Now—Smack!** (It's easier to remember a sentence than a strange set of letters.) Now construct a mnemonic sentence of your own to help you remember the temperature sequence of stars.

A Growing Nova

enough for this to happen. And when two stars do pass each other, they are usually moving so fast that their gravity can barely even slow them down.

Astronomers now believe that when two stars *form* close enough together, there is a good chance that they will settle into a stable orbit around each other. The big clouds of gas and dust that create stars are so huge that they form hundreds or even thousands of separate stars. Many of these stars must be fairly close together, or we would not find so many binary and multiple star systems in our sky.

One of the most surprising things astronomers have discovered about binary stars is that in some of them, a "river" of hot gas flows from one star to the other. This happens when the outside of one star is pulled away by the gravity of its companion. This gas forms a ring around the companion star, like water swirling around a drain as it empties. The gas builds to a critical level and then—FLASH!—it burns up all at once, producing an intense burst of light. This event is called a **nova** and it can make the binary star system tens of thousands of times brighter than usual.

If conditions in such a binary star system are just right, the transfer of gas from one star to the other can create a **supernova**. So much gas falls onto the star that it creates a runaway event, and the star dies in a gigantic nuclear explosion. A supernova can give off as much energy as 100 billion stars combined.

A supernova discovered in 1987: before (left) and after (right) explosion.

Supernovas send elements back into space, where they are recycled into new generations of stars and planetary systems. In fact, many of the elements found on Earth were created in supernovas.

WHAT IS A CLUSTER?

Some stars have not just one or two companion stars, but hundreds or thousands of fellow stars. These groups are called **clusters**. Viewed through a small telescope, a star cluster can sparkle like a box of glittering jewels.

We have seen that stars form inside a huge cloud of gas. When enough stars start shining, they produce enough energy to blow the rest of the gas cloud away. When the cloud disappears, the bright collection of new stars becomes visible. Clusters containing up to a few thousand young stars are called **open clusters** (or **galactic clusters**). There are a few obvious examples of them in our night sky, including the Pleiades (PLEE-uh-deez) and the Hyades (HY-uh-deez).

The Pleiades, often called the Seven Sisters, are a cluster of stars that form the left shoulder of the constellation Taurus. Alcyone, which is a thousand times brighter than our Sun, is the brightest star in the Pleiades.

About 160,000 light-years away from the Sun, the LMC globular cluster, Hodge 11, contains stars as old as some of the oldest globular clusters in our own galaxy.

Called a reflection nebula, this cloud of gas and dust particles (known only as IC 2220) shines by reflecting light from other stars.

There is another type of star cluster, called a **globular cluster**. The stars in a globular cluster are among the oldest in the galaxy. Globular clusters are tightly packed, like dense balls of stars. They contain from 10,000 to a million stars.

Open clusters got their name because they look more "open," or less concentrated, than globular clusters. Because they are put together more loosely, open clusters don't hold together very long. Over a billion years or so the stars in an open cluster will move apart. The Sun presumably formed in such a cluster five billion years ago but has since drifted away from its companions. Globular clusters, however, are so concentrated that they still have most of their original stars even after more than 10 billion years.

WHAT IS A NEBULA?

A **nebula** (plural: nebulae, pronounced NEB-yoo-lee) is a cloud of gas and dust particles spread across many millions of miles. It has all the material needed to be a star. (If it were squeezed into a small enough ball, it *would* be a star.) *Nebula* means cloud in Latin. Through the small telescopes astronomers first used four centuries ago, when Latin was the language of science, nebulae looked like faint smudges of light, or tiny clouds, in space.

There are several types of nebulae. **Reflection nebulae** shine by reflecting light from nearby stars. A nebula must have a lot of dust particles in it to reflect light in this way. Some

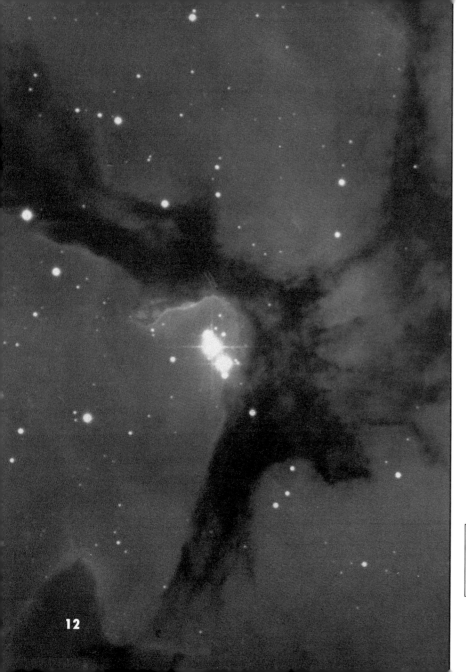

nebulae, called **emission nebulae**, shine on their own. In a gas cloud in which new stars are forming, the hot, young stars can emit so much energy that the gases in the cloud begin to glow. The cloud glows not because it is hot, but because it is fluorescing, much the way a neon sign fluoresces.

A single star can also create a nebula. A star near the end of its life may give off a shell of gas, like a cosmic smoke ring that expands outward into space. The star's energy keeps the shell glowing. These are called **planetary nebulae**, because through a small telescope the ring looks like the small disk of a planet.

Another way a single star can create a nebula is by exploding violently, becoming a supernova. A supernova shoots many billions of tons of material into space. This material gives off its own, fluorescing light. Over thousands of years, the gas cools and stops glowing. The shock wave from a supernova can also sweep up gas in the surrounding space and gather it into thin, glowing filaments—another way to make a nebula.

Finally, there are some clouds of gas and dust so cold and dark that they do not emit any visible

Found in the Sagittarius constellation, this emission nebula is called the Trifid stars. It contains stars whose energetic ultraviolet light causes the nebula to take on a red glow. It is about 3,000 light-years away.

A star may sometimes let out a shell of gas that looks like a smoke ring, causing a planetary nebula.

light. Because these **dark nebulae** block distant stars or bright nebulae from view, they make some starry parts of the sky look as though they have holes in them, with black, starless patches appearing in a starry field. We "see" dark nebulae only because they block the light from stars.

The Horsehead nebula in Orion is considered a dark nebula. It can only be seen because it creates dark areas in the sky, covering other stars.

WHAT IS A GALAXY?

All of the objects you've just read about—stars, binary and multiple stars, clusters of stars, and nebulae—can exist anywhere in the universe. But when you put them together in a single unit, you have a **galaxy**. Astronomers estimate that there are 100 billion or more galaxies in the universe.

Galaxies come in many shapes and sizes. Some are flat, spinning collections of stars and gas. Some are round, like big balloons. Sometimes two galaxies become connected, linking bright, starry arms with each other. Some galaxies are hardly bigger than a globular cluster; others are abnormally large.

Our home galaxy, which we call the **Milky Way**, is a fairly typical galaxy in terms of its size and shape. It contains more than 100 billion stars, mostly circulating in a big disk, shaped something

Our galaxy, the Milky Way, looks very similar to the Whirlpool Galaxy. Both are spiral galaxies.

like a Frisbee. An extra concentration of stars at the center gives the galaxy a central bulge. And, like bees buzzing around a hive, a small scattering

It is impossible to see the bright arms in some spiral galaxies, such as in this Needle Galaxy, because we see it edge on.

Our galaxy is called a **spiral galaxy** because its disk has several bright arms that spiral outward from the center. The arms are bright because within them nebulae are producing new generations of hot, bright, massive stars. The disk of the Milky Way rotates. All the stars and nebulae move in the same general direction but in their separate orbits, just as the planets of the Solar System orbit the Sun.

Our Sun is about 200,000 trillion miles from the central bulge of the galaxy, or about two-thirds of the way from the center to the outer edge. Moving at a speed of more than 500,000 miles per hour, it takes the Sun about 200 million years to complete one "galactic year"—that is, one orbit around the galaxy. This means that the Solar System is about 25 galactic years old, since it has completed the trip that many times since it first formed.

of stars—mostly members of the Milky Way's 200 or so globular clusters—make up the outer portions of the galaxy.

M 81

M 82

Shown here is a part of the sky in the constellation Ursa Major with two galaxies, M 81 and M 82.

The other principal type of galaxy is an **elliptical galaxy**. These galaxies have roundish shapes, ranging from nearly spherical to very stretched out and elongated, like a loaf of French bread. Some elliptical galaxies are very small, but others are the largest galaxies known, containing ten times the number of stars as contained in a spiral galaxy. The large elliptical galaxies are usually found near the center of a group of galaxies, and astronomers think they may have formed when several galaxies joined together millions of years earlier.

The Hubble space telescope, named after the American astronomer who first classified eliptical and spiral galaxies, was launched in 1990. It is the largest optical telescope ever put into space. At an orbit of almost 400 miles high, free of the Earth's atmosphere, the Hubble telescope has an unobscured view. It can see stars fifty times fainter and details ten times finer than any telescope on the Earth. One of the discoveries

An elliptical galaxy, the Leo I Dwarf Spheroidal galaxy was discovered by scientists only within the last 30 years.

Even though galaxies can contain billions and billions of stars, they are so large that they are mostly empty space, and the stars are separated by tremendous distances. If you were to use tennis balls as scale models of stars, you'd have to place them about 1,000 miles apart in order to represent the typical separation of stars in a galaxy. That adds up to a whole lot of nothing!

of the Hubble telescope is a **starburst galaxy** more than 230 million light-years away. A starburst galaxy is a group of star clusters resulting from the collision of two galaxies. The energy created is greater than 500 billion suns. In 5 or 10 billion years, the Milky Way may collide with other galaxies called the Large and Small Magellanic Clouds.

Stars are very small in comparison to the distance between them. Galaxies, on the other hand, seem to fill up space more completely. If you imagine that your tennis balls are the size of a typical galaxy, you'd only have to place them about 25 yards apart to show the distances between galaxies.

IMAGINING ASTRONOMICAL DISTANCES

It's hard to imagine the huge numbers that are used to describe distances in the universe. For example, how big is a million? Or a billion? How about a trillion?

One way to help imagine astronomical distances is to create a stack of ten pennies. Look at the size of the stack and then try to picture how high a stack of 100 pennies would be, then 1,000, then 10,000. How high would a stack of a million pennies be? Would you believe nearly a mile? A stack of a billion pennies would reach almost 1,000 miles high—about three times higher than the altitude of the space shuttle when it's in orbit around the Earth.

Astronomers don't deal in just millions or billions, but in trillions. The standard "ruler" used for measuring distances in the galaxy and beyond is the light-year, which is about 6 trillion miles long. A light-year represents the distance that a beam of light travels in one year. Light travels at a speed of 186,000 miles per second, which is the fastest known speed in the universe.

Light from the Sun takes eight minutes to reach the Earth, so we could say that the Sun is eight light-minutes away from us. The nearest star to the Sun is a little more than four light-years away. This means that the light we now see from that star is four years old, so we are seeing the star as it appeared four years ago. The Milky Way is about 100,000 light-years across, and the universe is thought to be about 15 billion light-years across. As we look at more distant objects, we look further back in time. As a result, astronomers can look into the night sky and see the history of the universe!

a billion pennies

three times the height of the Space Shuttle orbit

The constellation Cassiopeia is shaped like a "W" and can best be seen in the fall sky.

HOW TO OBSERVE THE SKY

2

To explore your home galaxy, simply go outdoors at night and look up at the sky. Some of the nebulae and unusual stars you can observe are best seen during particular seasons. So you may have to plan and wait before you can actually go out and observe them. And finally, it takes time to find your way around the heavens and learn how to scan the sky with binoculars or a telescope.

One of the first things you will notice is that some stars appear to form groups or patterns. In ancient times, stargazers played "connect the dots" with these stars and gave the resulting shapes special names. These groups of stars are called **constellations**. People named the constellations after animals or other familiar objects—whatever they thought the shapes looked like. This helped them to memorize the many stars in the sky. Today,

modern stargazers like you still use constellations to learn about the sky.

Sometimes the stars in a constellation are not actually close together in space. Some are closer to us and others are much farther away. But because they lie above us, they look close to one another in the sky.

The Big Dipper, which has seven stars in the shape of a ladle with a curved handle, is an easy constellation to find. It can be seen throughout the year from the Northern Hemisphere. The Big Dipper is actually part of a larger constellation called Ursa Major, which means Big Bear.

Knowing directions will help you find your way around the sky. The Earth's main directions—north, south, east, and west—are defined by the planet's spin. If you imagine Earth as a figure skater spinning on the tips of her ice skates, her head would be the North Pole and her feet would be the South Pole. Her outstretched arms would be like points along the Earth's equator, moving west to east. Because the Earth spins, it defines these directions for us naturally.

The audience sees the skater spinning around, just as we would see the Earth spinning around if we looked at it from distant space. But the skater could pretend that she is holding still and the audience is revolving around her. That's what we see here on Earth: it seems as though we are holding still and the sky is moving around us.

The Sun, Moon, and stars appear to rise in the east, cross overhead, and set in the west.

It took our ancestors thousands of years to understand that the sky holds still and the Earth itself spins, making it seem as though the Sun and stars rise and set.

Having learned directions, you now need to be able to measure distances in the sky. Astronomers use **angular distances** to make sky measurements. Angular distances are measured in **degrees**, based on the 360 degrees contained in a circle. If you face north, then turn around to face

TRY THIS ...

FINDING DIRECTIONS ON EARTH

It's easy to find which way is north. Go outside at about noon and stand so the Sun is at your back. Your shadow will then point to the north (if you live in the Northern Hemisphere).

But how do you find which way is north at night, when you don't have the Sun to help you? You look for the North Star! If you can find the Big Dipper, you can find the North Star. If you draw a line between the two stars at the front edge of the Big Dipper, it would point toward (but not exactly at) the North

The Big Dipper

North Star

pointer stars

Star. These two stars in the Big Dipper are called "pointer stars" because they point the way.

Once you have found north, you can locate east and west. Lie on your back with your head toward the north. Stick out your left arm

to the side, and it points to the east. Raise your left arm and sweep it toward your right side. Imagine the stars rising in the east and moving in the direction of your arm's motion, toward the west. It will take the stars about 12 hours to make the journey.

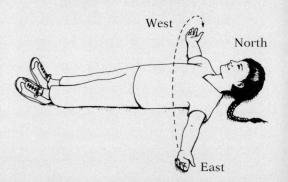

West

North

East

22

south, you have turned 180 degrees. Ninety degrees away from the **horizon** is the **zenith**, the point directly overhead. Use your hand as a "ruler" to estimate smaller angular distances.

When you have learned how to recognize certain constellations, find directions, and estimate distances in the sky, you will be able to find objects with the help of a **star chart**. Star charts show the

TRY THIS ...

MEASURING DISTANCES IN THE SKY

The width of the Moon as seen in the sky is half a degree. The width of a finger held at arm's length is about one degree. Do you think your finger can cover the Moon?

When the Moon is up, stretch out your arm and hold up one finger. Close one eye and compare the width of your finger to the size of the Moon. (You may find it easier to try this measurement during the day or at twilight, when the Moon does not seem so bright.) Your finger should appear about twice as big as the Moon. You now have your first ruler for measuring distances between stars.

Your fist held at arm's length spans about 10 degrees. Compare your fist to the width of the bowl in the Big Dipper. They should look about the same size (remember to close one eye).

Can you find another set of stars that looks about 10 degrees wide?

If you hold your hand at arm's length and spread your fingers out as wide as you can, it's about 20 degrees from the tip of your little finger to the tip of your thumb. The North Star is about 30 degrees from the two pointer stars in the Big Dipper. Can you measure this distance, using your fist and outstretched hand in combination?

1°

10°

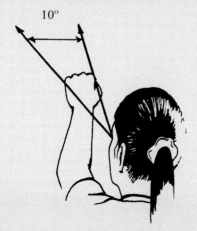

20°

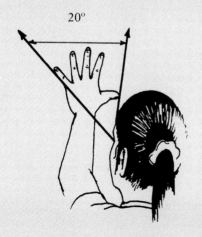

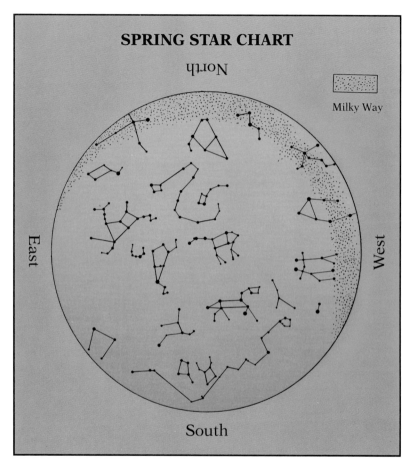

SPRING STAR CHART

North

Milky Way

East

West

South

distances between stars. With a little practice, you will be able to use a star chart as easily as you can use a road map. A typical star chart is shown here to help you get started.

A convenient type of star chart is called a **planisphere**. It has the entire northern sky on it (if it's made for the Northern Hemisphere, the area on Earth north of the equator), and a window that shows which heavenly bodies are in the sky at a particular time for any day of the year.

You can also use another important tool of astronomers, the **observation log**. In these logs, astronomers write the name of each object they study, the date, the weather conditions, and where they were when they made the observations, along with any special techniques that helped them find the object they were seeking. Try a notebook for your own observation log.

NAKED-EYE OBSERVATION

Before telescopes were invented, people used only their eyes to study the sky. This is called **naked-eye observation**. You can see many things in the sky using only your eyes. Constellations, for example, are best enjoyed with the naked eye.

When stargazing, it's important to find a place that's fairly dark. Why is that? Just because the Sun has gone down does not mean that the sky

major constellations and most of the bright stars in the sky. Astronomers use star charts in much the same way that travelers use road maps. While road maps use miles or kilometers to show distances between towns, star charts use degrees to show

is dark enough for viewing. Many people live in cities or towns where streetlights and buildings cast light into the sky. In big cities, the sky is brightened so much by electric lights that only a few stars can be seen. Even the Moon brightens the night sky, so much so that quite often faint objects like galaxies and nebulae cannot be seen.

Astronomers refer to the dimming of the night sky as **light pollution**. They have organized efforts worldwide to get cities to shield streetlights, billboards, and other outdoor illumination so the light does not shine into the sky and hide the magnificent celestial sights. To escape light pollution you need to stargaze far from city lights, or at least in a place where the lights are blocked from direct view. In a dark spot you'll be able to see hundreds of stars blazing in the night sky. To see especially faint objects, you should also plan your

TRY THIS ...

USING STAR CHARTS

Practice using your star charts to locate some constellations in the night sky. The chart on page 24 shows how the sky looks in the early evening for the spring. The top of the star chart is north, but notice that on the star chart the directions east and west are reversed from the way they look on maps of the Earth. Do you know why?

Pretend that you are lying on your stomach with your head to the north. In front of you on the ground lies a road map. On the map, east is to the right, just as your right arm is to the east, and west is to the left.

But what happens if you roll over on your back, keeping your head to the north? Suddenly east is to your left and west is to your right. This is the orientation astronomers use for their star charts. Astronomers are used to "thinking backwards" when they read star charts, and with a little practice, you will be, too.

Another thing to get used to is that star charts show the different brightnesses of stars as dots of different sizes. But the sky doesn't really look like that. You need to learn to recognize the patterns of the stars and use those as your guide.

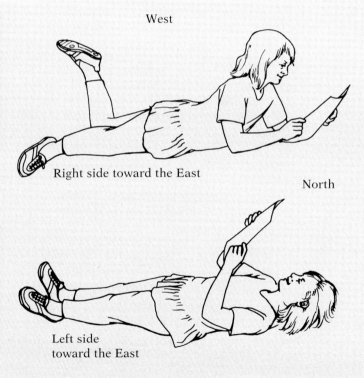

West

Right side toward the East

North

Left side
toward the East

TRY THIS ...

SEEING THE EFFECTS OF LIGHT POLLUTION

You can show the effects of light pollution by making a miniature night sky. Take a box—a shoe box will do—and poke some small holes in it. You can lay out the holes in the pattern of your favorite constellation and even enlarge some of the holes slightly to represent the brighter stars. When you are done, turn on a flashlight and put it in the box, then put the lid on. The light shining through the holes are your nighttime stars.

Take the box into a closet and close the door almost all the way. Don't lock yourself inside! Notice how bright the stars appear. Now open the door slightly and let some light into the closet. As the light strikes the outside of the box (which is like the Earth's atmosphere), do the stars seem to fade? Open the door all the way. Can you still see the stars? Take the box outside into the daylight. Now can you see the stars?

stargazing around the time of the new Moon, when the sky is particularly dark.

After you have found a dark spot, wait until your eyes have fully adjusted to the darkness. As your eyes adjust and become more sensitive, many faint stars will come into view. Another trick for seeing faint objects is to use "averted" vision. That means you don't look directly at the faint object. Instead, look slightly to one side of the object you want to see, and it will appear brighter. This works because it allows the light to fall on a more sensitive part of your eye.

It's a good idea to bring along a flashlight for looking at your star charts and writing in your observation log. You can dim your flashlight by covering it with a piece of red cellophane or plastic. There will be enough light so that you can see your charts, but not so much that the flashlight will be too bright for your eyes. Also, bring a chair or cushion that lets you lean back comfortably. If you stand and look up at the sky for very long, your neck will become stiff and you will tire quickly.

BINOCULAR AND TELESCOPE OBSERVATION

If you use a pair of binoculars or a small telescope, you can bring many objects into view that your eyes alone can't see. The openings on telescopes and binoculars are much bigger than the pupils of your eyes, so they can collect more light than your eyes can. They **focus** the light into an image you can see. Some telescopes, called **refractors**, use **lenses** to focus light (binoculars do, too). Other telescopes, called **reflectors**, use mirrors to focus the light.

Refractors were the first type of telescope to be invented. Simple magnifying instruments had been put together by lens-grinders in the 1500s.

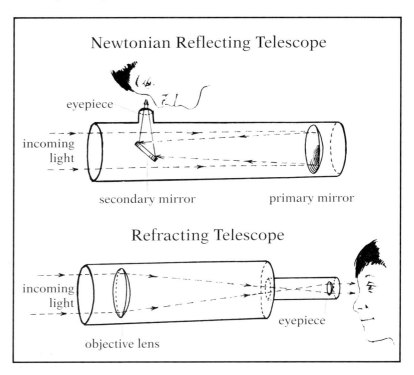

Newtonian Reflecting Telescope

eyepiece

incoming light

secondary mirror   primary mirror

Refracting Telescope

incoming light

eyepiece

objective lens

It was not until 1609 that the astronomer Galileo (1564-1642) assembled the first complete astronomical telescope and used it to study the Milky Way and other celestial bodies.

Refractors work in the following way: Light passing through a piece of glass changes direction, or is "refracted." If a glass lens is curved just right, the light will bend to form a concentrated, focused image. A simple refractor has a large lens called the **objective** and a smaller lens called the **eyepiece**. The two lenses work in combination to create an image that's the right size to enter your pupil. A reflector also uses a small lens for the eyepiece, but instead of a large lens for the objective, it uses a curved mirror, which bends

Galileo, standing, demonstrates his telescope.

and concentrates light just as a lens in a refractor does.

Telescopes and binoculars not only focus light into a bright image but also magnify objects. Most double stars, for example, look like a single point of light to your eye. But a pair of binoculars can magnify that point of light until it separates into two bright dots. The more powerful your binoculars are, the wider apart the two stars will appear.

Most telescopes for stargazing have a mount to hold them steady, but generally you hold binoculars with your hands. This means the binoculars will shake and give you a jittery image, since it is almost impossible to hold your arms perfectly still. One solution is to sit in a reclining chair that has arms. With your elbows resting firmly on the chair's arms, you will be able to hold the binoculars fairly steady.

A pair of binoculars is handy for "sweeping" the sky—exploring an area of the sky in a regular fashion by moving the binoculars slowly back and forth. Some areas of the sky, such as the Milky Way, are rich with interesting objects that you can spot best by sweeping.

This large telescope is mounted on a tripod to help keep it steady.

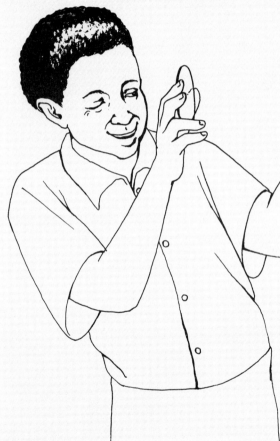

LEARNING HOW A TELESCOPE WORKS

You can demonstrate how a refractor telescope works with some simple hand lenses, which you can get at a local hobby or science store or through a mail order company. Ask for two lenses with different focal lengths: one about 10 to 14 inches, the other about 1 to 2 inches.

You can measure the focal lengths of your lenses at home. Inside, stand near a wall opposite a brightly lit window. Hold one of the lenses near the wall (don't block the window with your body). Move the lens toward and away from the wall until you form an image of the window on the wall. When the window's image is in focus, the distance between the lens and the wall equals the focal length of the lens. Measure the focal length of both lenses.

Notice that the size of the window's image is different for the two lenses. The lens with the longer focal length makes a larger image. You'll also see that the window's image is upside down. Lenses turn things upside down, and you have to get used to this when using some telescopes. (Binoculars include prism-shaped mirrors that turn the images right-side up again.)

With your two lenses you can now show how a telescope works. Let the lens with the longer focal length be the objective; the other lens is your eyepiece. Add the focal lengths of the two lenses together. The sum is the length of your telescope. Hold the two lenses apart at a distance about equal to the sum of their focal lengths. Now look through your eyepiece at your objective. When you get the spacing between the two lenses just right, you will be able to bring distant objects into focus. You have just made a telescope!

Notice that there is a very specific point at which the image comes into focus. Once you have the image in focus, try tilting the eyepiece. Does the image become distorted? The lenses in a telescope have to be very carefully aligned to get clear, sharp images.

NAMING A CONSTELLATION

In ancient times, astronomers from different countries developed different systems of constellations. They named the constellations after things they were familiar with. You can do this, too. Look at the night sky and pick out a group of stars. Use binoculars or a telescope or just use your eyes alone.

Draw a pattern of stars on a piece of paper or in a sketch book. Can you "connect the dots" to create a shape? Can you imagine any animal or object that resembles the pattern of stars you've picked? What name can you give your constellation?

Look up the names of the constellations, such as Orion, Perseus, Andromeda, Cassiopeia, Hercules, in books of Greek and Roman mythology to read fascinating stories. The Chinese and American Indians had different legends about the stars. See if you can find books of their myths.

The M 13 globular cluster can be found in the constellation Hercules from June to September.

OBSERVING THE NIGHT SKY

3

On any clear night you can step outside and, if you are in a place where the sky is reasonably dark, you can see more than two thousand stars with your naked eye. From a really dark site on a night when there is no Moon, so many stars will stand out that the sky may look completely unfamiliar to you. The constellations you know may seem lost among the crowd of glittering lights. This is the way the sky looked to people before electric lights were invented and before cities grew very large.

Some constellations are easy to pick out, even in a star-crowded sky, because the stars forming them are bright and are arranged in obvious shapes. Many constellations, however, are composed of ordinary stars that don't call attention to themselves. It takes practice in using a star chart to become familiar with these constellations and to learn to spot them quickly and easily. As you find your way among the different constellations, remember that most of the stars in a constellation are not really close to one another. Constellations are chance patterns of stars that serve as a handy system for organizing and remembering where things are in the sky.

For the most part, each star in the sky moves in its own path and at its own speed. It takes a long time before we notice this motion, because space is so vast. But as the stars move around, at some distant time in the future the constellations will be completely changed. For example, consider the stars in the Big Dipper. We see a Big Dipper shape just because we happen to be viewing the sky at this point in time. Over tens of thousands of years, the motions of the stars in this constellation will transform the shape of the Big Dipper. Our descendants will have to create a new set of constellation names to match future star patterns.

TRY THIS ...

LEARNING CONSTELLATIONS

There are a few constellations with which you should become familiar, because we will refer to them later when looking for some of our cosmic neighbors.

The following constellations are listed according to the seasons in which they are high in the sky in the early evening. The constellations do appear during the other seasons, but you might have to go outside at 3:00 A.M. to find them! Refer to your star charts to learn the shapes of the constellations, then seek them out.

SUMMER

Summertime is nice for stargazing because the nights are warm and comfortable. Also, because school is out, it might be easier for you to stay up later to watch the stars.

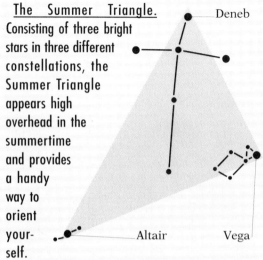

The Summer Triangle. Consisting of three bright stars in three different constellations, the Summer Triangle appears high overhead in the summertime and provides a handy way to orient yourself.

Looking to the south, you'll spot a bluish-white star centered between two fainter stars; this star is Altair, in the constellation Aquila (uh-KWIL-uh), the Eagle. Looking to the zenith, you'll spot the other two members of the Summer Triangle. The brightest star overhead is Vega (VEE-guh), in the constellation Lyra (LY-ruh), the Lyre. The final member of the triangle is Deneb (DEN-eb), which appears to the east of Lyra. Deneb is part of Cygnus (SIG-nus), the Swan.

Cygnus. The brightest stars in Cygnus, the Swan, also form the Northern Cross, which can be seen high overhead in the summer, pointing in a north-south direction. On closer inspection, you will see the extra stars beyond the cross that form the bent-back wingtips of Cygnus.

Lyra. Just west of Cygnus, a bright star will grab your attention. This is the star Vega, one of the brightest in the sky. Vega shines next to a parallelogram (which looks like a rectangle leaning over) formed by four fainter stars. These five stars are the brightest in the constellation Lyra, which was named after a stringed instrument called a lyre.

Many civilizations depicted this constellation as a bird, and some even represented it as a tortoise.

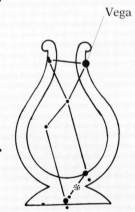

Kaus
Australis

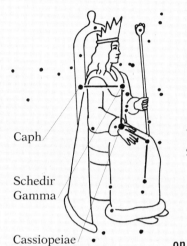

Sagittarius
(saj-ih-TAIR-ee-us) and

Scorpio (SKOR-pee-oh). As you look to the south, you will see this pair of constellations just above the horizon. Sagittarius, the Archer, holds a starry bow and arrow with which to shoot Scorpio, the Scorpion, whose stinger is curled and threatening. Part of Sagittarius forms a "teapot" shape that many people find easy to spot (the front of the teapot is the bent bow of the archer). If you live too far north, the horizon will block part of these constellations.

Antares

AUTUMN

Pegasus (PEG-uh-sus). This mythological winged horse is best found by looking for the four stars in it that form the Great Square. Because the square is very large and the stars forming it are not especially bright, you might overlook it at first. But once you've found it, you won't forget it.

In ancient Greek mythology, Pegasus was the magical winged horse who sprang full-grown from the neck of the Gorgon Medusa, when Perseus slew her. See page 48 for the constellation Perseus.

Markab
Scheat

Algenib
Alpheratz

Cassiopeia
(kass-ee-oh-PEE-uh). This constellation, whose five principal stars form a sort of squashed "W" (or an "M," depending on how you look at it), is on the opposite side of the North Star from the Big Dipper and about the same distance away. If you can easily spot the Big Dipper, you can use it to locate Cassiopeia. (During autumn, however, the Big Dipper will be low in the sky near the northern horizon. It might even be partially blocked by trees or houses, and therefore tough to spot.) Cassiopeia was a queen of Ethiopia in ancient Greek myths who angered the sea god Poseidon. Her daughter Andromeda was chained to a rock to be devoured by a sea serpent sent by Poseidon. Perseus rescued Andromeda and married her. Andromeda is also a constellation. Many Greek myths are remembered in constellations.

Caph

Schedir
Gamma

Cassiopeiae

WINTER

<u>Orion</u> (oh-RY-un). The Hunter is a familiar winter-time sight. In fact, you can't miss him! No other constellation has so many bright stars. Orion is marked by bright stars at his shoulders and knees, three stars across his waist that form his belt, and a glittering sword hanging below his belt. A special surprise lies in his sword, as we shall see on page 52.

In Greek mythology, Orion was a hunter loved by the goddess of the hunt, Artemis (Diana in Roman myths). He was chased to his death by a giant scorpion. Both Orion and the scorpion (Scorpio) were immortalized as constellations.

Betelgeuse
Rigel

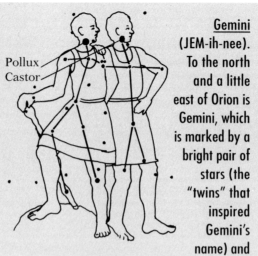

Pollux
Castor

<u>Gemini</u> (JEM-ih-nee). To the north and a little east of Orion is Gemini, which is marked by a bright pair of stars (the "twins" that inspired Gemini's name) and two lines of stars that are almost parallel. You can think of these two lines of stars as tracing out the figures of two stick men.

Eta Leonis
Algieba
Regulus
Denebola

SPRING

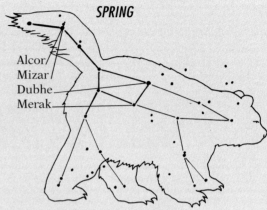

Alcor/
Mizar
Dubhe
Merak

<u>Ursa Major</u> (UR-suh MAY-jer). Within this constellation, the Big Bear, lies the Big Dipper. In the spring, when Ursa Major is high overhead, you can see the stars around the Big Dipper that mark the feet and head of this starry beast. At other times of the year, Ursa Major is low near the horizon in the early evening, so some of its stars can't be seen.

<u>Leo</u> (LEE-oh). The majestic lion lies south of the Big Dipper. Use the two pointer stars in the Big Dipper and go away from the North Star to find the Sickle. This is a curve of stars that looks like a backward question mark and represents the head and mane of the lion. A triangle of stars east of the Sickle marks the lion's hindquarters.

BUILDING A CONSTELLATION

By building a constellation, you can show that the stars within a constellation are not related to each other. You'll need a piece of stiff paper or cardboard, some string and tape, and some small round objects to represent the stars (perhaps some popcorn kernels or small buttons).

We'll use the Northern Cross in Cygnus as an example. Place a mark on your paper for each star in the Northern Cross, following the layout of the constellation shown on page 34. Number the star at the top of the cross as 1, number the stars on the crosspiece as 2, 3, and 4, and number the star at the bottom of the cross as 5. Poke a hole through the paper at each star position and run some string through each hole. Adjust and cut the length of each string coming through the holes as follows, and then fix each string with tape so its length cannot change:

Star 1—one inch
Star 2—ten inches
Star 3—four inches
Star 4—eight inches
Star 5—six inches

When the string lengths are properly adjusted, tape a "star" at the end of each string. Now hold your constellation board above your head and let the stars hang down toward you. Some of the stars are much farther away than others. But if you close one eye, it will seem as though all the stars are the same distance from you—which is the way they appear in our night sky. The stars are all so far away from us that they are mere points of light in the sky, and we cannot perceive their different distances.

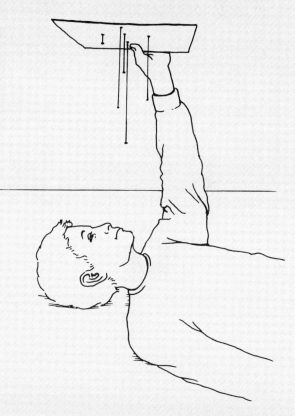

SPECIAL STARS

The stars we see in the night sky are special. They are not the most typical stars in the Milky Way. Most of the stars we can see with our naked eye are especially bright ones, which means they are very hot, very big, or both. Because these stars are very bright, they tend to dominate our night sky. When astronomers began studying space with telescopes, they could count and measure stars too faint to see with the eye. They discovered that the most common stars in the Milky Way are small, cool ones. These stars are very faint, and only a few can be seen with the naked eye.

Let's consider just how special some of our "night lights" are. If you look carefully at the stars around the sky, you might notice that they have different colors. That's not just an illusion— different stars really do shine with different colors. Stars of different colors are different temperatures.

Hot stars (classes O, B, and A in the system described in Chapter 1) burn with an intense, blue-white fury. Medium-temperature stars (F and G), like the Sun, give off a golden-yellow glow. The coolest stars (K, M, R, N, and S) emit a dim, red glimmer.

This photograph captures three constellations—Cygnus, Lyra, and Aquila—as well as the Northern Cross and the Summer Triangle. The stars Deneb, Vega, and Altair form the Summer Triangle.

It's not surprising that some of the brightest stars in the sky are the really hot ones. But it's also true that there are several cool, red stars that are bright in our sky. Astronomers have learned that these red stars are not nearby; the reason we can see them is that they are huge! What they lack in temperature they make up in size, so the total amount of light they emit is great.

To view some of these notable stars, you only need your eyes and clear skies. A pair of binoculars or a small telescope will make the colors seem more intense.

Summer

Vega, the brightest star in the constellation Lyra (and one of the stars in the Summer Triangle) is an A-type star distinguished by its bluish light (see the illustrations on pages 8 and 34). It is 55 times brighter than the Sun and only 26 light-years away—which is pretty close in a galaxy 100,000 light-years wide. Astronomers recently discovered that Vega is surrounded by a ring of dust and debris, which they think could be the leftovers from material that formed into planets orbiting Vega.

Arcturus (ark-TOOR-us) may be a cool K-type star, but it's also a giant star. It is about 30 times

—Vega

Lyra the harp with Vega

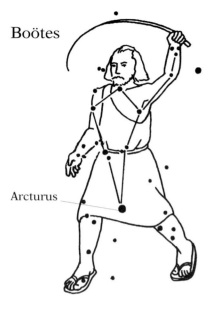

Boötes

Arcturus

bigger across than the Sun and more than a hundred times brighter! Arcturus is within the constellation Boötes (boh-OH-teez). To find this star, follow the curve of stars in the handle of the Big Dipper away from the dipper. Continue that curve from the last star in the handle for a distance about equal to the width of the Big Dipper, and you'll spot the orange-yellow Arcturus, shining to us from 36 light-years away.

The brightest star in Scorpio (see the illustration on page 35), Antares (an-TAR-eez), is more than a giant, it's a supergiant! This bright, orange-red star is seven hundred times bigger than the Sun. If we could place Antares at the center of our Solar System (that is, where the Sun is now), Mercury, Venus, Earth, and Mars would all be inside the star! Even though Antares is a cool M-type star, it gives off nine thousand times more light than the Sun does. But Antares contains only about ten or fifteen times as much material as the Sun—it's just puffed up to an enormous size.

Winter

Sirius (SEER-ee-us), in the constellation Canis Major, is the brightest star in the sky and shines with a bluish-white light. To find Canis Major, follow the three stars in Orion's belt (see the illustration on page 36) toward the southeast. Sirius is a fairly normal class A star, only a little hotter than the Sun and only 25 times brighter. But because it is less than nine light-years away, it commands a lot of attention.

Following a line through Orion's belt toward the northwest, you'll bump into Aldebaran (al-DEB-uh-ran), with its strong orange glow. Aldebaran is a cool K-type star in the constellation Taurus. It's

.–Antares

40

Antares in the constellation Scorpio

classified as a giant star, but it's not all that gigantic. This star is about 50 times bigger than the Sun and 180 times brighter. Aldebaran is 68 light-years away from us.

Orion offers two bright stars, Betelgeuse (BEET-ul-joos) and Rigel (RY-jel) (see page 36 for the illustration). Betelgeuse gleams with a reddish-white light in Orion's shoulder, and Rigel is a bright, bluish-white star in the leg of the Hunter, below the belt.

Canis Major

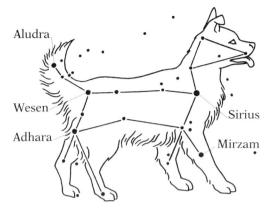

Taurus

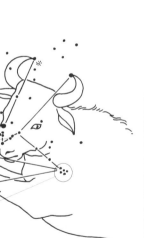

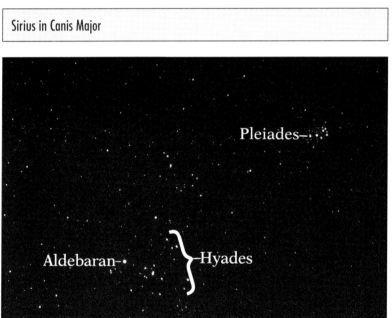

Sirius in Canis Major

Taurus, including the Hyades and the Pleiades

TRY THIS ...

BUILDING A SPECTROSCOPE

Astronomers have learned about each star by making a **spectrum** from its light. An example of a spectrum is a rainbow, which is the light from the Sun spread out into all its different colors.

Because starlight is so faint, astronomers have to use very sensitive spectroscopes to make a spectrum from it. Once they have made a spectrum from a star's light, they can carefully measure all the different colors and determine the star's temperature, chemistry, and size.

You can build a spectroscope that can make a spectrum of a few bright objects. You'll need a **diffraction grating** (available in the form of a transparent slide from a local science store or from a mail order company, such as Edmund Scientific). A diffraction grating is a specially produced piece of plastic that can split light up into its separate colors the way a prism does. You'll also need a small tube from a paper towel roll, some thick paper, and some tape. Cut a thin slit about an inch long in the paper (thin enough that light does not shine through it). Tape this paper over one

end of the tube with the slit centered on the tube's opening. Over the other end of the tube, tape the diffraction grating.

Put the end of the tube with the diffraction grating to your eye and look at various lights. Try a lamp and a fluorescent light in your house. At night, try different types of streetlights around your town. Look at the full Moon. For each light, you should see a thin

spectrum on each side of the slit. Can you describe the spectrum you see for the different lights? Is it a continuous band of colors like a rainbow, or are there only one or two colors?

Astronomers have very sophisticated spectroscopes for analyzing starlight, but the principle behind these tools and your spectroscope is the same.

Betelgeuse is one of the brightest of the supergiant stars. It's a class M star, like Antares, and it would also swallow the orbit of Mars or even Jupiter if it were in the Sun's position. Betelgeuse is nearly 14,000 times brighter than the Sun. That's why we can see it plainly, even though it is about 500 light-years away.

Rigel puts most other stars to shame. Even though it is twice as far away as Antares, Rigel appears brighter in our sky. Rigel is a B-type star, so it is hot, and it is *also* a supergiant. The combination makes Rigel 60,000 times brighter than our Sun! To produce this tremendous outpouring of light, Rigel has to consume its nuclear fuel at the rate of 80 billion tons a second.

STAR SYSTEMS

You probably won't have any trouble proving to yourself that stars in the sky have different colors. But to really drive the point home, you can inspect some double stars. When you look at two different-colored stars that are right next to each other, their colors will stand out more.

Besides being pretty to look at, binary stars can offer us important information about the universe. By measuring the motions of the two stars

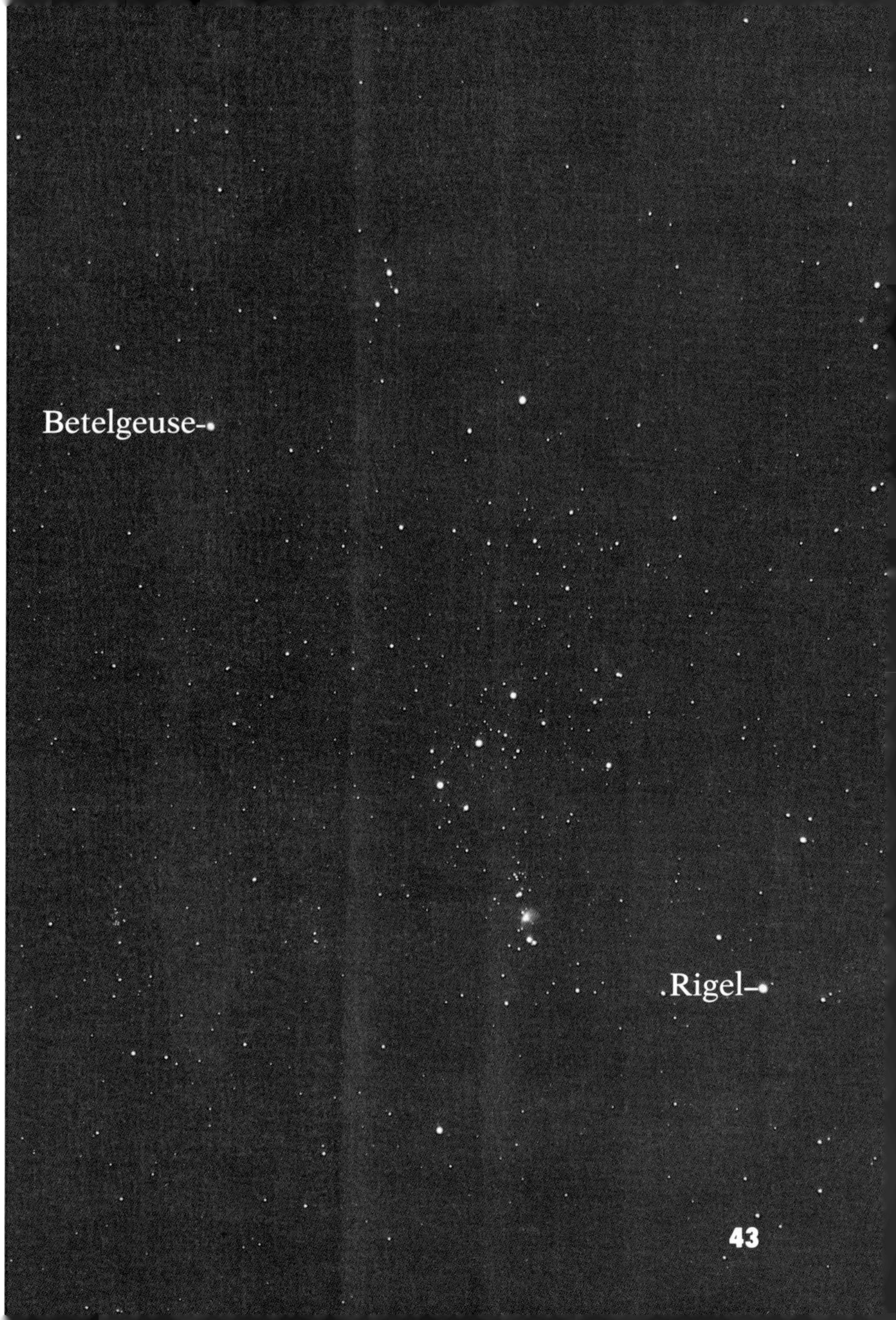

Betelgeuse and Rigel within the constellation Orion

Betelgeuse-•

Rigel-•

Companion Star   Black Hole

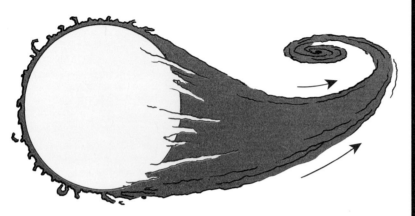

as they orbit each other, astronomers can calculate how massive (how heavy) the stars are. For single stars, astronomers can only guess at the mass.

  Astronomers can find a **black hole** only if it is part of a binary system. A black hole is a collapsed star that has become so small and dense that its gravity is intense. Nothing, not even light, can travel fast enough to escape from a black hole. Thus, a black hole is invisible. If a black hole has a companion star orbiting it, however, astronomers

This computer-enhanced photograph, taken by NASA's Hubble Space Telescope, shows the nearby spiral galaxy M 51. The somewhat spherical blue core of the galaxy has a black "X" at its center. The "X" marks the position of a black hole, which may be responsible for the intense radiation of this galaxy. The size of this image is 1,100 light-years.

regular star too faint to see.

Using this same method, astronomers try to deduce whether any planets are orbiting nearby stars. Planets give enough of a tug on a star to shift its position slightly. Unfortunately, the star moves such a tiny bit that astronomers are still arguing about whether anyone has actually proved that a star other than the Sun has a planet orbiting it.

STAR CLUSTERS

Once you've studied some of the star pairs and other star systems, it's fun to look at even bigger groups of stars—star clusters, which you read about in Chapter 1. As we saw earlier, these groups of stars may include from a few hundred to a million or more star members. Each group formed from a single cloud of material.

Open Clusters

There are two splendid open clusters to observe in the winter sky, both of which can be seen with the naked eye. Both can be found in the constellation Taurus (see the illustration on page 41). To find Taurus in the sky, follow the curve of the stars in Orion's belt to the star Aldebaran. Notice that Aldebaran is part of a small, V- shaped group of stars. This group, called the Hyades,

can look at the motion of the companion star and calculate the mass for the double-star system. In this way, they can determine whether the invisible member of the system is in fact a black hole or a

TRY THIS ...

SPOTTING DOUBLE STARS

You can spot a few double stars with the naked eye—this is a good test of your eyesight and of the observing conditions. Usually, though, you'll need a pair of binoculars or a small telescope. In some binary star systems, the stars are so near to each other that you would need a large telescope to see them as two individual stars. Sirius is a good example. The main star in this famous double star is much brighter than its companion, and the two are very close together. It takes a large telescope and special observing conditions to separate these two stars.

Listed here are a few of the binary stars that you can separate, or "resolve," using binoculars or a low-power telescope.

Albireo (al-BEER-ee-oh). Albireo appears at the head of Cygnus (or, if you prefer, at the foot of the

Albireo

Northern Cross!). The stars in Albireo are close to one another in brightness, but they differ markedly in color. One star appears orangish and the other bluish, and they should stand out easily when viewed through your binoculars. These two stars orbit one another once every 100,000 years!

Mizar (MY-zahr). This star is the middle one of the three stars in the handle of the Big Dipper. Most people can spot Mizar's companion, Alcor (AL-kor), with the naked eye. In Arabic astronomy, the two stars are known as "the Horse and the Rider." In England, they are known as "Jack and his Wagon." If you can't see both stars with your eye alone, a quick glance through the binoculars will show them clearly. And if you study Mizar with a telescope, you'll notice that it is itself a double star! Mizar is a true double alone, while with Alcor it is an optical double.

Alcor
Mizar

The Double-Double. If you look at the bright star Vega in Lyra, you'll notice a faint star next to it, above the parallelogram. On closer study, and with steady skies (a night when the stars are not "twinkling"), you'll be able to

see that this faint star is actually two stars of roughly equal brightness. If you can't see them with your naked eye, look through your binoculars and the dual stars will become clear. Each of these stars is itself a double star, which you can see through a big enough telescope. This is the famous Double-Double. Within each pair the two members orbit one another, and the two pairs themselves orbit each other every million years or so.

Double-Double

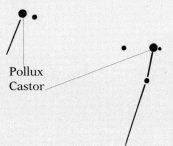

Pollux
Castor

Castor. This is the blue star of the twins in Gemini. You'll need a small telescope and very steady skies in order to separate the two brightest components of the star system Castor. A third, very faint companion orbits nearby. Each one of these three stars also has a companion (which can't be seen even through a big telescope), so there are six stars in all for this busy star system.

formed about 500 million years ago. Astronomers calculate that it will probably hold together for a billion years before the stars wander apart. The Hyades cluster has about 300 members. Aldebaran itself is not a part of the cluster, but it provides a handy marker for finding it. The stars of the Hyades cluster are about 130 light-years from us, or nearly twice as far away as Aldebaran.

If you keep following the line from Orion's belt through Aldebaran, you'll quickly reach the Pleiades (see the illustration on page 41). This cluster, which contains from five hundred to one thousand stars, is thought to be less than 50 million years old. Photographs taken through a big telescope show wispy remnants of the cloud from which the stars formed. The Pleiades are also known as the Seven Sisters, although most people can only see the brightest six stars with the naked eye. (This is another good test of your eyesight!) In Japan, the Pleiades are known as the Subaru (just like the car). Through binoculars, the sight of the Pleiades is a real treat. This glittering collection of bright, young stars is about 400 light-years away.

In the springtime you can look for the Beehive cluster, also known as M 44 (because it was the forty-fourth object recorded in a catalog compiled by Charles Messier in 1781). This cluster is easily seen with the naked eye under good observing conditions. Although the Beehive can be found in the constellation Cancer, that constellation

—Mars

The Beehive cluster, with the planet Mars at left

Cancer

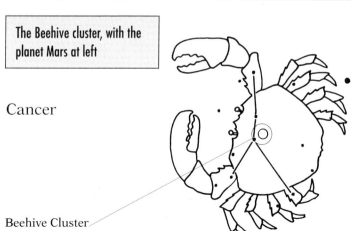

Beehive Cluster

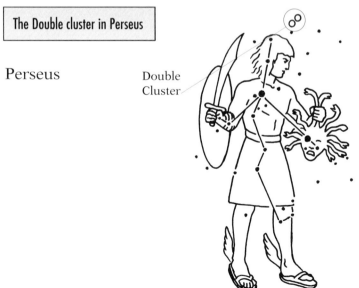

The Double cluster in Perseus

Perseus

Double
Cluster

is very faint, especially for a city dweller. A better way to find the Beehive cluster is by drawing an imaginary line between the star Pollux (PAHL-uks) in Gemini (the yellow "twin") and the star Regulus (REG-yuh-lus), the bright star at the base of the backward question mark in Leo. The Beehive cluster is along this line at a point about midway between Pollux and Regulus. This cluster offers a nice variety of orange and bluish stars. The Beehive Cluster is about 400 million years old and 500 light-years away.

In autumn you can explore the famous Double cluster (see the illustration on page 46), two separate open clusters in the constellation Perseus (PER-see-us). About 7,000 or 8,000 light-years away and somewhere between 5 million and 50 million years old, these clusters can be seen with the naked eye, even on an average viewing night. To find the Double cluster, you can use two stars in Cassiopeia as pointers. If you study the Double cluster through binoculars, look for some red stars in one of them; this is the older cluster. Each cluster contains more than 300 stars.

So far, astronomers have discovered about 400 open clusters, all of them in the disk, or flattened part, of the Milky Way. (There are undoubtedly many more such clusters, but they are hidden from view by the gas and dust in our galaxy.) Once you have become familiar with the ones presented here, you can search out others on a star chart and go hunting for them.

M 22, a globular cluster in Sagittarius

Globular Clusters

Because globular clusters are much farther away than open clusters, they are harder to find. Globular clusters are also so old—billions of years old—that they contain no bright, young stars. Astronomers know of more than 100 globular clusters. A few of these are visible to the naked eye as faint, fuzzy spots, but for most of them you'll need to use binoculars or a telescope.

An average globular cluster is about ten times bigger across than an open cluster, but with *ten thousand* times more stars. Through a small telescope, however, all this combined starlight appears as only a small patch of light.

In the summertime, find the globular cluster M 22 in Sagittarius by looking first for the star at the top of the "teapot" in Sagittarius (see the illustration on page 35). M 22 is just to the northeast of this star. The cluster appears as a starlike object to the naked eye, though it is difficult to see. Aim your binoculars or telescope at this "star" and you'll see a faint patch of light.

On a very dark night, and using averted vision, you can see that M 22 spreads out over a faint circle that's almost half the size of a full Moon. This smudge of light is generated by about 500,000 stars that are 10,000 light-years away from us. All of these stars are jammed into an area only a

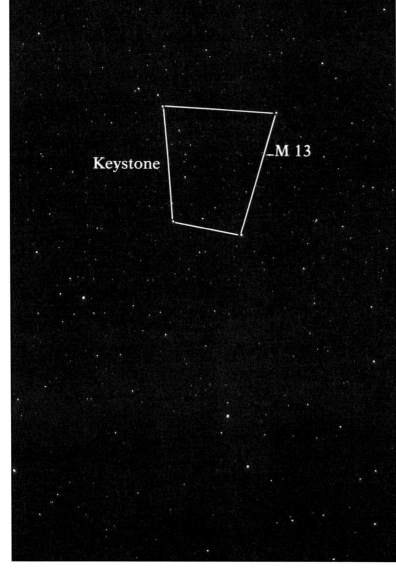

Hercules

little bigger than that occupied by the Pleiades, which contains only a few hundred stars.

One problem with viewing M 22 is that it is far to the south and generally appears close to the horizon. As you look toward the horizon, the atmosphere becomes murkier and it can hide faint objects like this cluster.

For stargazers in the Northern Hemisphere, there's another globular cluster that is more easily viewed. This is M 13, which is about 25,000 light-years away from us and contains a million stars. M 13 can be found in the constellation Hercules (HER-kyoo-leez), which lies between the bright stars Vega and Arcturus.

Hercules itself has no bright stars to distinguish it, which also means that there are no easy guides for locating M 13. At the center of Hercules are four stars known as the Keystone, which together form a trapezoid about ten degrees across (the width of your fist, as you learned in Chapter 2). Find the two stars on the

Hercules

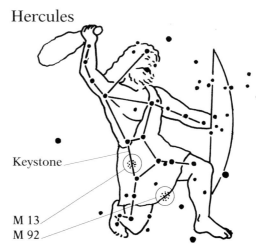

western edge of the Keystone. Draw a line between these two stars and look a little north of the midway point of this line. On a good night, you will be able to see M 13 with the naked eye. It will appear as a fuzzy-looking star.

TOUGH-TO-OBSERVE OBJECTS

Once you move away from stars and constellations and start hunting for fainter objects such as nebulae and galaxies, your job becomes a little more difficult. Review all the tips we described earlier for looking at faint objects. Dark skies are very important for observing nebulae and galaxies. Even so, there are some easy objects to start with, and the directions provided here will help you to locate some of the tougher ones.

Nebulae

The biggest nebula to look for, and one that you need only your eyes to enjoy, is the Great Rift. If you go out in the summertime and look overhead, you can find the constellation Cygnus winging its way along a milky-white stream of light. This stream is called the Milky Way—the same name as our galaxy. The faint band of light is created by millions of stars within our galaxy that are too distant to be seen individually. (People in ancient times thought the band of light looked like spilled milk, and so they named it the Milky Way. Polynesian people thought that this band of light looked like the white belly of a shark, and so they named it after this feared creature.)

If you look closely at the Milky Way on a dark night, you'll see what look like dark ribbons dividing it into two parts. This

EXPLORING THE MILKY WAY

With your binoculars, scan the Milky Way along Cygnus and work your way south toward Sagittarius. You'll be able to see that the Milky Way is composed of innumerable faint stars. Explore the dark bands of the Great Rift nebula. When you look toward Sagittarius, you are looking toward the very center of the Milky Way, about 30,000 light-years away.

Found in the Milky Way, the Great Rift looks like dark ribbons dividing the galaxy in half.

long, dark break is the Great Rift. It is created by thick clouds of gas and dust that lie in the galaxy's disk and block the light from distant stars. Early astronomers thought these dark areas were holes in the galaxy, but we now know these are just places where we can't see the background stars.

Once you've gotten a feel for the "big picture" by viewing the Milky Way, you can home in on a smaller, individual nebula. The best time is during the winter, when the constellation Orion is well placed for viewing. Focus on the "sword" formed by three stars hanging below Orion's belt (see the illustration on page 36). Look at the middle star in the sword. Does it look special in any way?

It may not look special at first, but if you aim your binoculars at it you'll find that it is not a star at all, but a glowing patch of sky. This is the famous Orion nebula. It's a small, luminous portion of a much bigger cloud that is cold and dark. Within the cloud, hundreds of new stars are being created. The entire gas cloud covers most of the sky outlined by the constellation Orion, and in time much more of the area will glow with new stars. The part we can see now—the glowing gas of the Orion nebula— spans about 15 light-years.

The Orion nebula was formed by a small

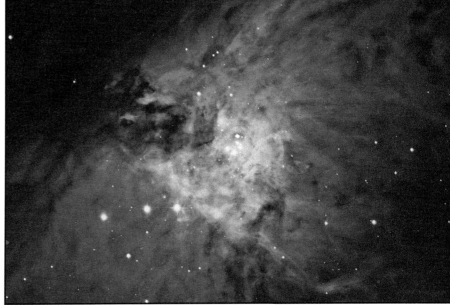

The Orion nebula, the first nebula ever photographed, is the closest bright nebula to Earth. Because it is only 1,300 light-years away, astronomers know more about it than any other nebula.

The large central star of the sword of Orion is actually a group of four stars known as the Trapezium cluster. These stars are expected to live about 10 million years or so.

group of hot, newborn stars. The powerful winds given off by these young stars have blown a hole in the outer edge of the large gas cloud, opening a "window" through which we can look. Through the window we see a small cluster of stars and the gas it has caused to glow. The central stars in the nebula are a mere 300,000 years old. On a human time scale, that's about equal to a two-month-old baby. With a big enough telescope you can see four bright stars, a group called the Trapezium (truh-

PEE-zee-um). These stars have expected lifetimes of just 10 million years or so.

The Lagoon nebula, like the Orion nebula, is a cloud of gas in which stars are forming. On a dark night you can see a patch of light from this nebula. Looking south toward the teapot of Sagittarius, start at the topmost star in the handle of the teapot, then draw a line toward the star at the top of the teapot's lid (see the illustration on page 35). Follow this line another step. Through

Trifid nebula

Lagoon nebula

As you observe the constellation Sagittarius, you may be able to see the Lagoon nebula, which is close to the archer's bow. The Trifid nebula, also near the bow, can't be seen without a telescope.

binoculars, you'll see a star with a cluster of faint stars on one side and the patchy cloud of the Lagoon nebula on the other. The Lagoon nebula has enough gas in it to make about one thousand stars.

There are other nebulae that are very different from the Orion or Lagoon nebulae. A planetary nebula, for example, is a circle of glowing gas surrounding a single old star. Planetary nebulae are much smaller than the nebulae we have looked for thus far, so get ready for some serious sky searching!

One of the most famous planetary nebulae is

The Ring nebula is found in the constellation Lyra.

the Ring nebula in Lyra (see the illustration on page 34). Using a small telescope, look directly between the two stars that form the bottom of the parallelogram in Lyra (the side farthest from Vega). This small, bright cosmic "smoke ring" won't look much different from a star. Use your averted vision to see whether you can make out a faint shape. (The star whose light makes the gas ring glow is too faint to see without a big telescope.)

Near the Ring nebula lies a larger planetary nebula called the Dumbbell nebula. It has a shape like a bow tie, which reminded early astronomers of a dumbbell weight. Like the Ring nebula, this is a cloud of gas that was belched into space by a star that is now too faint to see. It will be a challenge to your stargazing talents to find the Dumbbell. It lies in the constellation Vulpecula (vul-PEK-yoo-luh), which is not well known because it is so indistinct. A line drawn from Vega to the southwest through Albireo points toward the Dumbbell nebula. Extend the line about half as far again from Albireo as the distance between Vega and Albireo. The nebula is about one-fourth as big as the full Moon, but ghostly and faint.

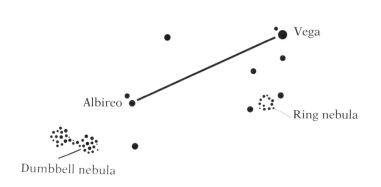

The Dumbbell nebula lies near the Ring nebula and is shaped like a bow tie.

DEATH OF A STAR

One of the most famous nebulae is the Crab nebula, in the constellation Taurus. It is the remnant of a star that exploded as a supernova. The Crab nebula can be seen with binoculars in very dark skies, but for best viewing you will need a small telescope. It's impressive to consider that this fuzzy little blob of light represents a cloud of gas and debris that is expanding more than 50 million miles each day.

The supernova was seen from Earth in the year 1054. Chinese, Japanese, Turkish, and American Indian stargazers recorded the appearance of what looked to them like a new star in the constellation Taurus. Writings, petroglyphs (drawings on rock), and illustrations on pottery were all used to show the star and the number of days it could be seen in the sky. These ancient stargazers wanted to make a record that would last, communicating to others how impressed they were by this event.

In 1987, a supernova appeared that was visible in the Southern Hemisphere. A new star shone brightly in the heavens for a brief time, the first supernova seen without a telescope in nearly 400 years.

If you saw a supernova and wanted to make a recording of it that would communicate everything you had observed and that would last as long as the records of the Crab nebula have, what kind of recording would you leave?

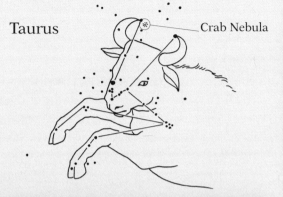

Taurus — Crab Nebula

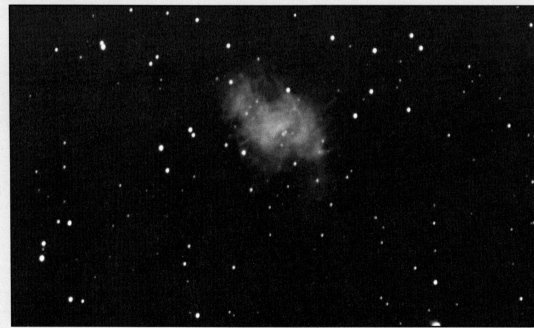

The Crab nebula was first seen by stargazers in 1054. It is expanding more than 50 million miles every day.

Galaxies

Galaxies are the basic building blocks of the universe. Astronomers estimate that the universe contains 100 billion or more galaxies—about the same number as there are stars in each galaxy. The galaxies are spread over the entire known universe, a volume of space about 100 billion trillion (100,000,000,000,000,000,000,000) miles wide.

Before about 1920, astronomers did not know that there were other galaxies like our own. In a telescope, distant galaxies appear to be small swirls of light. They do not look much different from nebulae, and in fact what we today know to be other galaxies were first called "spiral nebulae." Only when astronomers developed telescopes big enough to spot individual stars in these spirals did they realize that what they were seeing were huge, distant star systems—island universes.

People in the Southern Hemisphere can see two bright patches of light in the night sky. These are small, odd-shaped galaxies that orbit the Milky Way. These two satellite galaxies are called the Magellanic (maj-uh-LAN-ik) Clouds, because when Magellan sailed around the world centuries ago (from 1519 to 1522), his sailors brought reports of them back to Europe.

It's not unusual that the Milky Way has companions. Galaxies group together just as stars do. The Milky Way and the Magellanic Clouds belong to a collection of about 20 galaxies, called the Local Group. The Local Group is in turn part of a bigger collection called the Virgo Cluster, so named because when we look at the constellation Virgo we are looking toward the center of this cluster. The Virgo Cluster may contain more than one thousand galaxies, two hundred of which are considered bright.

WHAT NEXT?

Astronomy is one of the few sciences where people who are amateurs—that is, who pursue the science out of interest and don't make their living from it—can help do some important work.

For example, an amateur astronomer in Australia named Robert Evans has set a record for discovering supernovas in nearby galaxies. Evans scans nearby galaxies using a homemade 10-inch telescope. Because he has looked at these galaxies so many times, he has memorized the patterns of stars around each one. He notices immediately when a new dot of light has appeared. When this happens he alerts the professional astronomers, who turn their large telescopes on the supernova and begin a detailed study of it. Without Robert Evans's efforts, many supernovas would pass unnoticed.

Amateur astronomers also discover most of the new comets that pass through the inner Solar

System. Comets, which are mountain-sized chunks of frozen gases, ice, and rock, are of great scientific interest because they can tell us more about how the Solar System formed. Each year, one or two new ones are found.

There is also a worldwide network of dedicated sky watchers who monitor variable stars. The brightness of variable stars changes, increasing and fading repeatedly over time. These amateur astronomers keep track of variable stars and notice right away whenever any special activity occurs in one of them.

You can take part in some of these important scientific efforts. Or you can continue to explore the sky simply because it's fun. Looking up to the heavens helps you remember the specialness of this tiny ball of rock on which we live. It's fun to look at the sky and think that the stars you see are producing material that may someday form a system of distant planets. Nearly all the material that makes up the Earth was once part of stars that died billions of years ago. We truly are star creatures.

For your next step in exploring the galaxy, contact amateur astronomy groups in your area and find out when they set up their telescopes to share a view of the heavens with others. If you go to one of these "star parties," you can learn from people who already know their way around the sky and who have a variety of powerful telescopes. Amateur astronomers are often enthusiastic teachers of the various sights in the sky.

Your local science center or planetarium usually has telescopes and often schedules regular nights for stargazing. The planetarium can project the appearance of the sky for different seasons and help you to learn the various constellations. You can check the phone book for these organizations, or call the reference desk of your local library for information.

Odyssey (for kids) and *Astronomy* and *Sky & Telescope* are magazines for stargazers that you might enjoy reading. You will probably be able to find these at your library, or you can subscribe.

It takes time to learn your way around the sky and to find some of the wondrous objects we have described. But the time it takes is well spent. In looking at the lights in the night sky, you'll experience the history of the universe. The light can be hundreds, thousands, even millions of years old by the time it reaches the Earth. Every star or faint patch of light you see brings a special story.

OBSERVING OUR NEAREST GALAXY NEIGHBOR

Observers in the Northern Hemisphere are treated to the sight of the Andromeda (an-DROM-ed-uh) galaxy. In the autumn, when you are away from city lights, you can see this galaxy with your naked eye. Start by locating the Great Square of Pegasus. Look for a line of three bright stars that lead out from the square's northwest corner. From the middle of the three stars, look north (toward Cassiopeia) past one star to a second, fainter one. Andromeda is next to this fainter star.

The Andromeda galaxy is the most distant galaxy you can see without using a telescope. Though it may look like only a faint blob of light, it represents the light from *200 billion* stars. This light has traveled more than 2 million light-years to reach your eye.

You can see the Andromeda galaxy as a faint blur of light without a telescope. Its light comes from 200 billion stars.

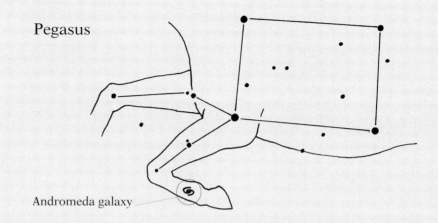

Pegasus

Andromeda galaxy

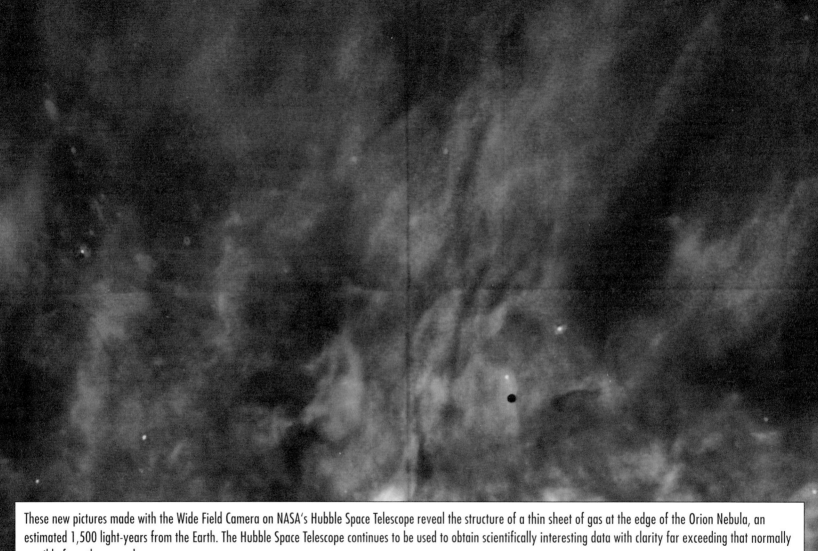

These new pictures made with the Wide Field Camera on NASA's Hubble Space Telescope reveal the structure of a thin sheet of gas at the edge of the Orion Nebula, an estimated 1,500 light-years from the Earth. The Hubble Space Telescope continues to be used to obtain scientifically interesting data with clarity far exceeding that normally possible from the ground.

GLOSSARY

angular distance The apparent size of an object or the apparent distance between two objects as measured in degrees.

binary star A system in which two stars orbit around a common center of gravity between them. Also called a double star.

black hole A collection of extremely dense matter, whose gravity is so strong that not even light can travel fast enough to escape it.

cluster A collection of stars. There are several kinds of clusters. A globular cluster is a group of up to a million stars, containing some of the oldest stars known. An open cluster (also called a galactic cluster) is a group of a few hundred to a few thousand relatively young stars found in the disk of a spiral galaxy.

constellation A pattern of stars in the night sky.

degrees A unit for measuring angles; there are 360 degrees in a circle.

dark nebula See nebula.

diffraction grating A device that splits an ordinary beam of white light into the various colors of the spectrum.

double star See binary star.

elliptical galaxy See galaxy.

emission nebula See nebula.

eyepiece A small lens that projects the image made by a telescope or binoculars onto the eye and magnifies that image.

focus The effect of a curved lens or mirror to concentrate a beam of light into a small, sharp image. The point at which such an image is formed.

galactic cluster See cluster.

galaxy A collection of stars, clusters, and nebulae held together by their combined gravity. Galaxies are the basic building blocks of the universe. There are two main kinds of galaxies. Elliptical galaxies range in shape from nearly spherical to elongated, like a loaf of French bread. Spiral galaxies have a flat disk of stars and gas that features two or more curving arms and a central bulge. A new galaxy recently discovered is the starburst galaxy, a group of star clusters resulting from the collision of two galaxies.

globular cluster See cluster.

horizon The line where the body of the Earth cuts off the sky from view.

image A representation of an object made by a lens or mirror.

lens A piece of glass shaped so that light passing through it is redirected to form a concentrated image.

light pollution Light from streetlights, buildings, and natural sources such as the Moon that brightens the atmosphere and makes it hard to see faint objects.

light-year The distance a beam of light travels through a vacuum in one year, equal to about six trillion miles.

matter The stuff of which the universe is made: solids, liquids, gases, or isolated atoms or particles.

Milky Way Our name for our home galaxy; also, the stream of light across the sky created by countless distant stars in the flat disk of our galaxy.

multiple star A system in which more than two stars orbit each other about a common center of gravity.

naked-eye observation Stargazing using only your eyes, without the aid of a telescope or binoculars.

nebula A cloud of gas and dust in space. There are several kinds of nebulae. A dark nebula is one that doesn't give off visible light. Dark nebulae are thick enough to block the light shining from the stars that lie behind them. An emission nebula, however, is hot enough to give off light. A planetary nebula is a ring or shell of glowing gas given off by a star. Planetary nebulae are so-named because, to early astronomers, the small circle of gas resembled a planet. A reflection nebula doesn't give off its own light, but it contains dust particles that do reflect starlight.

nova A star that flares up and brightens periodically.

nuclear fusion The process by which atomic particles are combined into new particles. During nuclear fusion, energy is released.

objective The light-gathering lens or mirror in a telescope.

open cluster See cluster.

optical double star A pair of stars that appear to be close together to the naked eye but actually are not. Optical double stars are not true binary stars.

planetary nebula See nebula.

planetarium A theater that re-creates the appearance of the night sky by projecting images of the stars and planets on a curved screen.

planisphere A star chart that can be adjusted to show what heavenly bodies are in the sky at any time of the year.

reflection nebula See nebula.

reflector A telescope that uses a mirror as its objective.

refractor A telescope that uses a lens as its objective.

spectrum The array of colors that results when a beam of white light is split into its component parts.

spiral galaxy See galaxy.

star A ball of hot gas that shines light; nuclear fusion keeps a star hot for most of its life. Stars come in various sizes, colors, densities, and temperatures.

star chart A "road map" of the sky, showing the positions of the visible stars.

starburst galaxy See galaxy.

supernova A powerful nuclear explosion within a star or a double star that can outshine a galaxy of 100 billion stars.

universe The collection of all the matter and energy that we know about or can learn of through science.

zenith The point in the sky directly overhead.

PHOTO CREDITS:

INDEX

A

Albireo 46
Alcor 46
   double star 7
Alcyone 10
Aldebaran 40-41, 45, 47
Altair (star in Aquila) 34,38
Andromeda constellation 35
Andromeda galaxy 59
Angular distances 22-23
Antares 40
Aquila constellation 34, 38
Arcturus 39-40
Astronomy magazine 58
Averted vision for seeing
   faint objects 27

B

Beehive cluster (M 44) 47–48
Betelgeuse 41, 43
Big Dipper 7, 21
Binary stars 7, 9–10, 43–44
   ways to spot 46
Binoculars 27
Black holes 4
Boötes constellation 40

C

Canis Major constellation 40, 41
Cassiopeia constellation 20, 35
Castor 46
Clusters of stars 10–11, 45–51
Color
   of stars 6
   and temperature of stars 38, 44
   of the Trifid stars 12

Comets 57–58
Constellations
   descriptions 21–24
   names of 31
   visibility and season of
     the year 34–36
Crab nebula 56
Cygnus constellation 34, 38

D

Dark nebula 13
Degrees for measuring
   distances 22–23
Deneb
   in Cygnus 34
   in the Summer Triangle 38
Diffraction grating 42
Directions on Earth,
   from positions of stars 22
Distances
   astronomical 19
   ways to measure 23–24
Double stars 7, 9–10, 43–44
   ways to spot 46
Double-Double 46
Dumbbell nebula 55

E

Elliptical galaxy 17, 18
Emission nebula 12
Evans, Robert 57
Eyepiece of a telescope 28

G

Galactic clusters 10
Galactic year 15
Galaxies 57
   description 14–18

Galileo 28
Gemini constellation 36, 48
Globular clusters 11, 49–51
   M 13, in Hercules 32
Gravity
   and formation of a nova 9
   and formation of a star 6–7
Great Rift of the Milky Way 52

H

Hercules constellation 32
   M 13 globular cluster in 50
Horizon as a reference point for
   distances 23
Horsehead nebula 13
Hubble space telescope 17–18
Hyades 10, 41, 45, 47

I

Image in a telescope 27

K

Keystone constellation 50–51

L

Lagoon nebula 53–54
Lenses
   binocular and telescope 27
   learning to use 30
Leo 48
Leo constellation 36
Leo I Dwarf Spheroidal galaxy 17
Lifetime of a star 7
Light pollution 25–27
Light-year 19
Local group of galaxies 57
Lyra constellation 34, 39–40

63